LONDON

HASTINGS

OSHAM

PEVENSEY

St VALERY-SUR-SOMME

DIVES

ROUEN

AYEUX

MANDY

KU-875-326

NORTHAMPTON COLLEGE
R39531A 0098

245.05

# The Bayeux Tapestry

# The Bayeux Tapestry

Norman Denny & Josephine Filmer–Sankey

## The Story of the Norman Conquest: 1066

Collins    London

THE LIBRARY
COLLEGE OF FURTHER EDUCATION
NORTHAMPTON

ISBN 0 00 195058 4

Text © Norman Denny and Josephine Filmer-Sankey 1966
Illustrations reproduced from photographs supplied
by Maison Combier, 4 Rue Agut, Macon, Saône-et-Loire, France
Endpapers designed by Dale Maxey
First published in Great Britain 1966
This reprint 1985
Printed and bound in Hong Kong by South China Printing Co.

# Introduction

The Bayeux Tapestry is a very old version of what we are apt to think of as a modern thing. It is a strip-cartoon, one of the earliest and certainly the greatest that is known to us, and it was made within a few years of the tremendous historical event it records: the Norman invasion of England, which took place just nine centuries ago.

The French still call it "Queen Matilda's Tapestry" – *La Tapisserie de la Reine Matilde*. Matilda was the wife of Duke William of Normandy, "William the Conqueror," and she became Queen of England after the Conquest. For a long time she was believed to be the designer and maker of the tapestry, but we now know that this was not the case. It was made to the order of Bishop Odo, William's half-brother, to be hung in Odo's Cathedral at Bayeux, a little town in Normandy some ten miles from the sea.

Bishop Odo ordered it to be made, but there is no reason to suppose that he had any share in its making. For the design, an artist was needed. We do not know who he was; but that he was a great artist is proved by the splendid life and vigour of his drawings, the skill with which he told the story, and the picture he has given us of the life of the time.

We must note an important point. The Bayeux Tapestry, although it is always referred to as such, is not really a tapestry at all. A tapestry is a cloth made on a loom, with its pattern or design woven into it. The Bayeux Tapestry is a piece of embroidery (needlework), the pictures being stitched in woollen threads of eight different colours on a long strip of bleached linen. The designer may have drawn them first on parchment, but it seems more likely that he drew them on the linen strip, which he then handed over to the craftsmen (or women) who did the embroidering.

It is an immense work. The strip of linen is about two hundred and thirty feet long and twenty inches wide. It was made in eight sections, afterwards stitched together, probably embroidered by separate teams of craftsmen. Nothing is now known of these people; but at the time when the work was carried out (probably between A.D. 1070 and 1080) there was a School of Embroidery at Canterbury, in Kent, which was famous throughout Europe for needlework of this kind. We cannot be sure, but it looks as though this is where the work was done. In short, although the tapestry is Norman in origin, and represents the Norman point of view, it was probably executed by English hands.

After its completion the tapestry was taken to Bayeux Cathedral, where it was preserved among the church's greatest treasures, being hung round the nave on feast-days and special occasions. There it remained for seven centuries, untroubled, meticulously cared for, and (it would seem) largely disregarded by the scholars and historians who might have been expected to take more interest in something that was at once a great work of art, a wonderful story and a unique historical document. Then more notice was taken of it, and its life became more adventurous. It narrowly escaped destruction in the early days of the French Revolution and later was taken to Paris to be exhibited there by order of Napoleon (who was planning another invasion of England at the time). During the next hundred years or so it underwent many vicissitudes and changed its dwelling many times, suffering considerable damage in the process. But in 1945 it was placed on exhibition in the former Palace of the Bishops of Bayeux, next to Bayeux Cathedral. Then, in 1983, it was again moved. After examination and meticulous restoration it was installed in a splendid new home, the sumptuously converted Centre Guillaume le Conquerant in the Old Seminary.

Unlike the modern strip-cartoon, the tapestry has no conversation and does not make use of those interesting bubbles saying, "*Thinks* –." The

Latin inscription gives us some indication of what is going on, but for the most part the pictures are left to speak for themselves. There are many gaps, and many of the details are so puzzling that learned men have been disputing over them for the past hundred years, and will no doubt continue to do so. The tapestry does not explain; sometimes it seems to contradict itself, and sometimes, as we know from other historical records, it gets things wrong.

In writing about it we have adopted a particular plan. The first paragraph on every page (where there are two paragraphs, as there generally are) simply describes what is happening. By reading these first paragraphs alone you will be able to follow the story as the tapestry tells it.

But where necessary we have added a second paragraph in smaller type, often much longer, in which we look more closely at the picture and discuss some of the details. We try to explain things more fully, to fill in something of the historical background, and, where the truth of the tapestry is in doubt, to point to what is probably, or possibly, true. But we cannot pretend that this is not partly guesswork. We are dealing with a very old story buried deep in the past.

And if you are to understand the story you must carry your imagination back into the past – to that remote medieval world in which chivalry and barbarism were so strangely mingled. It was a world of devout faith in God, which held honour and loyalty to be the highest values, while at the same time it practised treachery and intrigue, and every kind of brutality. The working of the medieval mind is illustrated in the way the tapestry depicts King Harold. He was the villain of the drama, as the Normans saw it, but he is never treated as a bad man. On the contrary, he is treated with respect, as a great and gallant man who offended against God by breaking his solemn oath, and paid the penalty. He is a noble figure; and it is this feeling for the nobility and dignity of man which makes the Bayeux Tapestry the great work of art it is.

*N.D.*

*J.F.S.*

POSTSCRIPT. One very small scene has been omitted from this account of the Bayeux Tapestry. It contains two figures, those of a woman called Aelfgyva and a monk. Its meaning and significance are lost to us. There is a theory that it has to do with William's offer of his daughter in marriage to Harold; but this is unsupported by any evidence. In short, the scene is a puzzle for scholars, and since it contributes nothing to the story, except a moment of confusion, we have felt justified in leaving it out.

**It seems certain** that some years before this opening scene Edward, who was childless, had promised Duke William of Normandy that he should succeed him on the throne of England. Possibly Harold was sent to confirm this promise. But it may be that he went of his own accord to gain the friendship of William; for these two were renowned warriors, great and powerful men. The year was probably 1064. There are certain things we must remember about the Tapestry. First, that it is a tale founded on rumour and report, the tales men told at the time, which must often have been altered in the telling. Much of the truth is now lost to us. And secondly it is a Norman tale—told, that is to say, from the Norman point of view and pointing a moral, as we shall see as the story progresses.

EDVVARD REX · V

**The story begins** in the Royal Palace of Westminster.
Edward the Confessor, the King of England, is talking to Harold, Earl of Wessex, his wife's brother.
He sends Harold on a mission to Normandy, in France.

Harold leaves for the coast with a hawk on his wrist,
a pack of hounds and men-at-arms following behind.

The hawk and hounds indicate that Harold was engaged upon a mission of peace; and the hawk was also a token of nobility. At the right of the picture we see the first of the trees which appear at intervals throughout the Tapestry, both as a decoration and to separate certain of the scenes. Trees figured frequently in the decorative designs of the period; but these may also point to the Norman origin of the Tapestry. The Normans, although they had settled in France, were Norsemen, men from the North; and the tree is part of Nordic mythology—Yggdrasil, the Tree of Life.

Harold and his men enter the church at Bosham, on the Sussex coast, to pray for a safe voyage.

Then they go to one of Harold's many homes, the Manor House at Bosham,

where they feast and make merry until a servant hurries up the stairs to tell them

that all is in readiness for their departure.

They would have had to hurry off, taking advantage of wind and tide.

Bosham Church still exists, but we are not to suppose that it ever looked much like the building in the picture. The Tapestry "suggests" buildings, but does not seek to show them as they were. It suggests that Harold's house was big and important by giving it a colonnade and a flight of stairs leading to the Great Hall. Nor does the Tapestry take account of time. Boats sailed with difficulty in those days. They may have had to wait many days for a fair wind.

The borders contain beasts both real and imaginary, scraps of old fables, scenes of country life. For the most part they are only a decoration, but now and then the story flows over into them, and sometimes they make their own contribution to it.

Stripping off their woollen hose they wade out to the boat, which men hold with poles to prevent the tide from leaving it stranded. Harold goes first, still carrying his hawk. A man in the boat is setting up the mast.

S:VENTO:PLENIS VE-
NIT:INTE RR A:
VVIOONIS
COMITIS

The ships sail across the English Channel, packed with Harold's escort of armed men, whose shields are arranged along the sides. The ship behind is steered by Harold himself with the kind of rudder they used in those days, which was like an oar. In the ship in front a lookout has climbed to the masthead, a man is sounding with the lead, and another is making ready the anchor as they approach land.

HAROLD: hIC:

These are ships similar to those in which the Vikings sailed. The Tapestry is much nearer to truth in its ships than in its buildings. The Vikings were accustomed to slinging their shields along the side of the vessel when it was under sail and the oars were not in use.

The English land, and Harold is taken prisoner by Count Guy de Ponthieu,
a vassal of Duke William, who rides down to the seashore leading a force of mounted men.
Harold is defending himself with his saxe, a weapon which was both a dagger and a knife,
used for eating as well as fighting.

Tales differ as to this landfall. The Tapestry shows the English wading
calmly and peaceably ashore. But many historians believe that they were
shipwrecked or at least driven ashore by adverse winds. The place was near
Saint Valéry at the mouth of the river Somme, in Guy de Ponthieu's
domain. It is unlikely that Harold would have wished to land there, since
Count Guy was unfriendly towards him, as the story shows.

THE LIBRARY
COLLEGE OF FURTHER EDUCATION
NORTHAMPTON

REM: ET IBI EVM: TEN VIT:

They ride to Count Guy's castle of Beaurain.

Harold goes in front and Count Guy follows with their retainers.

The English have been disarmed, but the Norman men-at-arms carry their spears.

It was the Age of Chivalry, when good manners and brutality went hand in hand. A nobleman who became the prisoner of another nobleman was commonly held to ransom. But Harold is treated with the respect due to a great lord. He rides in front disarmed but still carrying his hawk. As a rule the Normans can be distinguished from the English in the Tapestry by the fact that they are clean-shaven, with the backs of their heads shaved in the Norman style; whereas the English are shown with a full head of hair and a moustache. But sometimes the Tapestry forgets about this.

VBI:hARO LD: ⅂VVIDO:PARABO LANT:

The Castle of Beaurain. Seated in his great chair, Count Guy tells Harold
of the ransom he must pay to be released from captivity.
On the right an Englishman is listening to their talk, peeping cautiously round a column.

The scene is filled with drama. The group of retainers on the left, both
English and Norman, anxiously await the outcome of the bargaining.
Harold's sword has been returned to him, which suggests that the negotia-
tions are going well; he is being treated with honour. A soldier touches
Count Guy's arm to draw his attention to the approach of someone from
outside. The Englishman by the pillar peers and listens, and perhaps it is he
who escaped from the castle to bring Duke William news of what has
happened. We must remember that the Tapestry plays tricks with time.
All these things, which may have taken days or weeks, are packed into
one scene.

UBI·NUNTII·WILLELMI· DUCIS·VENERUNT·ADWIDO NĒ

TUROLD

Messengers arrive from Count Guy's overlord, Duke William of Normandy.

Count Guy receives them with his battle-axe in his hand, while a dwarf holds their panting horses.

They have come to demand the surrender of Harold, and they are followed by

armed riders sent by the great Duke to escort the English nobleman to his castle.

The second of the messengers, it seems, was called Turold. We know nothing about him; but since his name is mentioned, we must suppose that he was a person of importance. Count Guy, if we may judge by his attitude and his battle-axe, was not pleased at receiving this order; but it was one that he was bound to obey. The building is another representation of his castle. The dragons on the riders' shields were an emblem common to both Normans and English.

NVN TII : VVILLELMI

The scene has changed to Duke William's castle at Rouen,

and now we learn how the Duke came to hear the news of Harold's capture.

William sits listening to the tale told by an Englishman who has escaped from the

Castle of Beaurain, perhaps the man we saw peeping round the pillar.

So much may be surmised, but it is not easy to account for the man in the
tree, who perhaps belongs to the previous picture and was waving goodbye
to the departing riders.

We see opposite the meeting between William and Harold.

William has ridden out to greet his guest.

Count Guy, riding ahead, introduces the two mighty men.

WIDO: AD DVXIT HAR OLDVM ADVVILGELMVM: NORMANNORVM

This is the first of the great and solemn occasions depicted in the Tapestry. These were two lords and warriors renowned throughout Christendom. Harold was the most powerful man in England, after the King; and William, by his success in Normandy and his victories over the rival dukedoms of Brittany and Maine, was already known as "the Conqueror." They were destined to become friends and, later, deadly enemies.

The place was the town of Eu, on the boundary between Ponthieu and Normandy. Count Guy is riding a strange-looking horse which some people believe to be a mule. Certainly it is unlike any other in the Tapestry.

NNORVM: DVCEM

Harold and William ride together to Rouen, Harold going in front, in the place of honour.

A watchman hails them from the tower of the castle as they approach.

Then, in the Great Hall, William sits listening while Harold addresses him.

It may be that he is delivering a message from King Edward.

The picture makes it clear that this was a formal interview of great importance. Harold, who is weaponless, speaks with eloquent gestures, while William listens intently, clasping his sword. But the two men must have had many such conversations in the months that followed, during which Harold was William's guest—and also his prisoner, if William chose to treat him as such. Whether Harold was there as Edward's ambassador, or whether he had come solely on his own account (or both) there was much for them to discuss: above all the future of England and Normandy, and the part each was to play in the affairs of their respective countries after Edward's death. We have no record of what passed between them. All that can be said with certainty is that in the course of this visit, which seems to have lasted for at least a year, Duke William of Normandy and the Earl of Wessex became firm friends—for a time.

HIC·DVX·VVILGELM·CVM HAROLDC

O·VENIT·AD PA
LATIV SVV

Duke William leads his army against Duke Conan of Brittany, who has declared war on him.

William, carrying a mace (a battle-club and symbol of authority), rides with two knights in armour

and other mounted men; but he himself wears only a quilted tunic and no helmet.

Harold accompanies the expedition. The army crosses the river Couesnon,

between Normandy and Brittany, passing near Mont Saint-Michel, St. Michael's Mount,

which is to be seen in the background. Here Harold performs a feat of great valour.

He rescues two soldiers from the quicksands at the river's edge and carries them safely ashore.

:ADMONTE MICHAELIS ET HIC TRANSIERVNT FLVMEN COSNO HIC HAROLD DVX TRAHE DEARENA

That they should have gone campaigning together is clear evidence of the friendship between William and Harold. Here, for the first time in the Tapestry, we see a "gonfanon," the square battle-pennant with three points, attached to the lance of one of the knights. These pennants were of Nordic origin, another reminder that the Normans were men from the North.

The war against Brittany.

The Normans attack the castle of Dol, and Duke Conan escapes by sliding down a rope.

Going in pursuit of him and his army, the Normans pass by the town of Rennes,

which we see in the background, with its Latin name "Rednes."

VER ... TIT:· HIC MILITES ... WILLE

RED...NES

Here the Tapestry is in error. Duke Conan was not in the castle of Dol when it was besieged. The truth is that he was besieging it, since the Breton lord who held it (by feudal right under Conan) had allied himself to William and risen against his overlord. The Norman army went to the relief of the castle, and, having driven off Conan's army, pursued it past Rennes. The castle of Dol was one of the "motte and bailey" kind—a fortress built on a hill (the "motte") with rings of outer defences consisting principally of earthworks. The open spaces between these outer rings, where troops could manoeuvre, were known as the "baileys." Since Dol is shown as having a drawbridge it must also have had a moat. The artist has decorated the two hills, those of Dol and Rennes, with pictures of birds and beasts.

Duke Conan has taken refuge in the Castle of Dinan.

He is fiercely assailed by the Normans, and they set fire to the castle.

We see him offering the keys of the town to Duke William on the end of a lance,

in token of surrender.

A complicated scene in which there is much action. The Tapestry shows us the Castle of Dinan in a double sense: on the one side it is being attacked and on the other side it is capitulating. The setting fire to the castle is a separate scene in itself. It is carried out by two armoured knights, each of whom has put down his shield and thrust his lance with its gonfanon into the ground. Since the work was done by knights and not by ordinary soldiers, it was evidently a feat calling for great skill and daring.

THE LIBRARY
COLLEGE OF FURTHER EDUCATION
NORTHAMPTON

WILLELM: HAROLDO: HIE VVILLELM VENIT BAGIAS VE

William "gives arms" to Harold—

that is to say, he does him honour for the gallant part he has played in the fighting.

Then they ride to the Castle of Bayeux.

The giving of arms was an important matter. William was conferring a high honour on Harold, just as in the present day a man who has done his country a distinguished service may be made a Knight of the Garter, or awarded the Order of Merit or the Congressional Medal of Honour. But in the feudal age it had a double meaning; for if it conferred dignity and privilege, it also required something in return—allegiance. We see the significance of this in the scene that follows.

Opposite, Harold swears allegiance to William. Standing with his hands upon an altar and a chest containing sacred relics (they are believed to have come from the Cathedral at Bayeux), he utters a solemn vow that he will be William's "man," and serve and obey him in everything.

BI HAROLD:SACRAMENTVM:FECIT:/ HIC HAROLD:DV
VVILLELMO DVCI:-

The gravity of the occasion is manifest in every detail of the scene. William sits on his ceremonial chair, sword in hand, extending one hand with a pointing finger as though to say, "Swear!"; and the gesture is reflected by the man standing on Harold's other side. This solemn moment is the turning-point of the story, and it depicts an event of great significance in the history of western Europe. That Harold swore an oath of allegiance to William is not in doubt; it implied, among many other things, that he would not accept the Throne of England without William's consent. Did he swear willingly? That is the question. The Tapestry (of Norman origin, we must remember) would have us believe that he did, that this was a free oath freely taken, arising out of the friendship between the two men. But Harold was in William's hands. William could hold him captive and threaten him with death if he did not swear.

Harold returns to England.

In a house ashore, which may have been his own Manor House of Bosham, people await his coming.

ADANGLICAM:TERRAM :·ET VENIT:AD:EDVVARDV· REGE

Harold rides to London.

He is the man on the black horse and we see that he has shaved off his moustache.

He goes to the Palace of Westminster to tell King Edward of his adventures in Normandy.

What did Harold tell Edward? He had been away from England for more than a year and some report of his doings—of fighting in Brittany, of hunting, feasting, and carousing in friendly company with William—must have reached King Edward's ears. The news can hardly have pleased the King because he badly needed Harold in England. The situation had changed in the past year, and Edward may well have realized that any promise he had given William of succession to the English throne could no longer be fulfilled without bloodshed. Harold's attitude, as he crosses the cobbled yard of the Palace, is that of a man preparing a speech in his defence. We do not know if he told Edward of his oath of allegiance to William.

HIC PORTA TVR : CORPVS : EADWARDI : REGIS : AD : ECCLESIAM : SC PETRI AP

The Tapestry here moves from right to left; we do not know why. The artist may have felt that he achieved a more dramatic and moving composition in this way; and perhaps he wished to lay stress upon the splendid new church, which Edward himself had built, and which was destined to outlive so many kings. There is a great wealth of detail. The picture of Westminster Abbey (as we now call it) is the only one in the Tapestry where an attempt has been made to depict the real appearance of a building. We see a man fixing the weathercock, in indication of the fact that work on the building was still not complete; but the Hand of God pointing down from Heaven shows that it has been consecrated. In fact, the ceremony of consecration was performed exactly a week before Edward's death, on the 5th of January, 1066. The Tapestry depicts his funeral bier with great care and reverence.

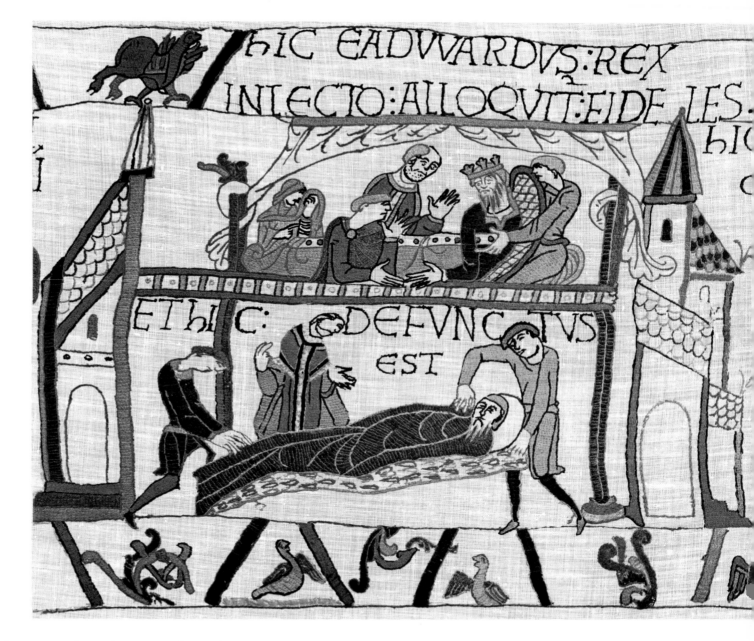

HIC EADWARDVS REX
IN LECTO ALLOQVIT FIDE LES
ET HIC DEFVNCTVS EST

Another year has passed, and King Edward the Confessor is dead. We see him above lying on his deathbed in an upper room of his Palace of Westminster, speaking his last words to Queen Edith, his wife, while a priest and an attendant minister to him. He is laid in state in the Great Hall below and then is borne, in a solemn funeral procession, to the newly built Church of St. Peter, which later became the Abbey of Westminster.

DEDERVNT: HAROLDO: ORO[C]NA: REGIS hIC RE[S]IDET: hAROLD REX: AN[GLORVM]: GLORVM: STIGANT ARCHI[E]PS

Harold is offered the crown of England in succession to Edward the Confessor. He stands, axe in hand, looking at the crown and perhaps wondering if he should accept. He does accept, and in so doing breaks his solemn oath to William of Normandy. We see him seated on the throne, crowned and holding the orb and sceptre which were, as they still are in England, the symbols of monarchy. Beside him stands Archbishop Stigand proclaiming the new ruler to the people, who listen and applaud.

We must again remember that the tale told by the Tapestry is a history of events seen through Norman eyes. The breaking of a solemn oath was a gross offence against the laws of chivalry, the gravest of sins in the eyes of the Christian Church. To the Normans, to William of Normandy, there could be no extenuation of this; and the Tapestry suggests none. Harold was not only forsworn, he had betrayed his friend. That is the grim story as the Tapestry tells it. Moreover Harold's acceptance of the crown incurred the wrath of the Church for another

reason. Archbishop Stigand, who proclaimed him to the people and may possibly have performed the ceremony of Coronation (of this we cannot be sure), had been excommunicated by the Pope and therefore was not entitled to hold the office of Archbishop. Such was the case which caused powerful forces to be arrayed against Harold, whose defence was that he had taken the oath under duress, being in William's power, and that therefore it was not valid.

A strange star appears in the sky, a comet with a fiery tail, and the people gaze at it in terror. An astrologer tells Harold that this is an omen of misfortune. In the border below this scene we see the ghostly outlines of ships stealing across the sea. Perhaps this was Harold's dream as he lay troubled by the thought of the oath he had broken and the doom which might follow the breaking of his oath.

The comet was Halley's comet, which can be seen from the Earth at intervals of about 75 years. It would have been clearly visible in the English sky in February of that year, 1066. We shall next see it in the year 1984.

A boat sails from England with messengers
bringing William news of Harold's coronation.

The scene is bordered by a tree on either side, two Nordic Trees of Life, as
though to stress the momentousness and gravity of this secret mission. The
messengers may have been Norman or English, for there were powerful
men in England who were hostile to Harold.

Opposite, William holds a Council of War. He has been robbed of
the English crown by Harold, and he resolves instantly to seize it by
force of arms and to exact retribution for Harold's betrayal. He gives
orders for a fleet of ships to be built to carry his army across the
Channel, and men at once set to work felling trees for their timbers.

HIC : WILLELM DUX : IUSSIT
NAVES : EDIFICARE :

William is seated at the Council of War, with his hand on his hip, and beside him is Odo, Bishop of Bayeux, William's half-brother and principal adviser (it was he who later ordered the making of the Tapestry). We are not to suppose that William's decision to invade England was taken as quickly as the picture suggests. Ambassadors were sent to England to remind Harold of his oath and calling upon him to surrender the crown to William. Harold refused. If William believed that Harold had betrayed him, Harold believed no less sincerely that his oath, taken under the threat of force, was not a binding one. He also knew that his surrender of the throne would lead to civil war in England. We must try to understand this conflict in the spirit of the time. These were two honourable men, according to their lights, despite the deadly quarrel that now divided them.

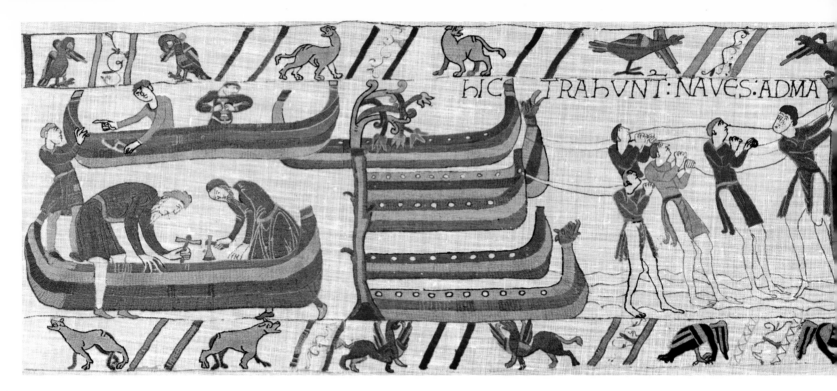

HIC TRAHVNT: NAVES: ADMA

The building of the invasion fleet. Craftsmen with axes, adzes, and such other tools
as they used in those days are finishing off the planks and timbers.
The vessels are then dragged down from the building yards to the sea.

The place where the work was done was probably Dives-sur-Mer, on the
Normandy coast not far from the town of Caen. The building of this great
armada within a few months was in itself a very remarkable feat. Some
eight hundred vessels must have been needed to transport William's powerful and well equipped army.

Opposite, the loading of the ships. Arms and supplies are being carried on board:
hauberks (suits of mail), spears, swords, helmets, barrels of wine and water, and sacks of flour.

While this great work of preparation was going on in
Normandy, Harold was no less busy in England raising and
preparing a fleet and army of his own to meet the coming
invasion. And for both commanders the same problem
arose, that of keeping their forces together. Both were de-
pendent to a large extent, although not wholly, upon feudal
levies—serfs and villeins bound by feudal law to give armed
service to their lords. But the laws were strict and clear: the
men were only obliged to serve for a limited time. Moreover they were peasants, men with fields to till and families
to support. They were likely to grow restless, and even
mutinous, if they were not allowed to go home for the
harvest.

William leads a party of his knights down to the foreshore to embark in the ships.

William here accomplishes another remarkable feat. This was the first time in western Europe that an invading army had taken its horses with it. The earlier invaders of England—Picts, Scots, Angles, Saxons and Romans—had landed on foot and scoured the countryside for horses; but William's armoured knights needed chargers specially bred and trained to carry them. This body of knights constituted the most formidable part of William's army, one that the English did not possess. Altogether the force may have amounted to as many as two thousand knights, but by no means all of these were Normans. William could call upon the services of some eight hundred knights in his Dukedom of Normandy. The rest were from other countries, adventurers for the most part who had been induced to join him by the promise of rich rewards when England was conquered. His foot soldiers, including many trained archers, may have amounted to another four thousand men. It was a great and powerful army for those days, although not as numerous, and in certain respects not as well trained, as the force which Harold was capable of raising.

+ hIC:WILLELM:DUX INMAGNO:

NAVIGIO:    MAR E    TRAN

The invasion fleet crosses the English Channel, sailing from Saint Valéry to Pevensey, the ships tight-packed with men and horses. William's ship is towards the front, with a signal lantern at its masthead and on its sternpost a carving of William's son Robert, blowing a horn and carrying a spear with a gonfanon.

William sailed from Saint Valéry at the end of September, having moved his armada from Dives two or three weeks earlier. The wind played a great part in these events, frustrating both commanders. Harold had assembled a powerful fleet off the Isle of Wight with which he planned to attack William from the sea while his ships were still being completed; but the wind failed him. Later William fretted and fumed waiting for a favourable wind to take him to England; but the delay as it turned out was greatly to his advantage, for in the meantime Harold has been forced to send his ships to the Thames to refit. This was one of the reasons why the Norman army was able to land unopposed.

SIVIT ETVENIT AD PEVENE SÆ:·

hI

There was no resistance to the Norman landing. Harold, with his splendid force of house-carles, reputed to be the finest foot soldiers in Europe, had been obliged to proceed in great haste to the north, to encounter a new trouble that had befallen him. Harald Hardrada, King of Norway, had arrived at the mouth of the Humber with a powerful army, accompanied by Tostig, Harold's brother. Their aim was to conquer the Kingdom, over which Tostig was to rule as the vassal of the Norwegian King. Harold met them at Stamford Bridge, having covered two hundred miles by forced marches. He defeated them after a hard battle, but only at the cost of heavy losses. William's army landed in the south while this was going on. No doubt Harald Hardrada and Tostig took advantage of the threat of a Norman invasion to attack when they did, but there was no alliance between them and William.

William's armada lands on the English coast, at Pevensey in Sussex.

The vessels are beached, the masts unshipped, and men and horses come ashore,

Mounted men set out to scour the countryside for possible enemies and for supplies.

The Normans, spreading eastwards along the coast, pillage the countryside for food.
They round up sheep, cows, and pack horses.

The knight Wadard, to the right of the picture, was evidently a person of importance, since his name appears above him on the Tapestry ("Hic est Wadard"). But although there are many theories, we know nothing positive about him.

The Norman cooks are here preparing a feast for William
and his high officers to celebrate the army's successful landing.
It seems that the cooking was done in the open air. On the
left of the picture we see two cooks boiling meat in a big pot
suspended over a fire on forked poles. Above is a row of
chickens on spits. Next is a baker standing by his oven and
using a large pair of tongs to transfer the cooked loaves or
cakes to a trencher. The food is then taken indoors and passed
along to a serving table made of shields laid over trestles.
Behind this table is a man blowing a horn to announce that
the meal is ready.

William and his nobles are seated at the festive board. It was probably a round table, but its shape has been altered so as to fit in the figure of the serving man bearing a great dish in the foreground. The central figure at the table is Bishop Odo, who seems to be blessing the feast, although no one is paying much attention to him except William, seated on his right. Three of the noble lords have already started their meal and a fourth is apparently drawing their attention to something. On the right of the picture William is conferring with two of his leading advisers, Bishop Odo on his right and Robert Mortain, who was also his half-brother.

ISTE:IVSSIT:VTFO DERETVR:CASTELLVM:AT·HESTENGA CEASTRA

Orders have been given for a fortress to be built, and we see this on the right of the picture. It was probably a wooden stockade on a mound surrounded by a deep ditch, with a number of watchtowers where lookouts and archers could be posted. The workers all appear to be Normans, although one might have expected English peasants to be rounded up to do the digging and carrying. The Normans for the most part are working hard under the supervision of their officers, but discipline seems to have been a little lax, since two of the men are fighting. This was probably an important episode at the time, but we do not know what it was about.

HIC:NVN[T]LATVM EST: WILLELMO DE HAROLD: bIC DOMVS:IN CENDITVR: HIC:M

On the left of the picture is William receiving an urgent report from one of the scouts who have been sent out to keep watch for Harold. Then we see the Normans burning a house and forcing a mother and a child to flee from their home. Next comes a tall building, which represents the town of Hastings, with its great door open for the Normans to sally forth. Lastly, on the opposite page, we see William making ready to lead his army into battle. A groom brings up his charger.

This series of short scenes is like a quick sequence in a cinema film. The designer of the Tapestry, who was above all things a storyteller, is building up the suspense before the grand battlepiece which is to follow. William, on the left is for the first time holding the Papal Banner with its four points. This had been consecrated and sent to him by Pope Alexander II, and it is inserted here to show that the expedition had the blessing of the Church. Nothing is now known about the burning of the house, which again may have been an incident of special importance at the time

…MILITE IS: EXIERVNT:DE hESTENGA:

William rides out at the head of his knights, the shock troops that were the most powerful part of his army. From now on he may be recognized by the mace, which he carries throughout the battle. The date was the 14th of October, 1066.

AD PRELIVM: CON TRA: HAROL DVM REGE HIC VVILLE

THE LIBRARY
COLLEGE OF FURTHER EDUCATION
NORTHAMPTON

Two scenes separated by a clump of trees. On the left a messenger named Vital rides up to William, having come from one of the parties of mounted men sent ahead to watch Harold's movements from the hilltops. The armies are now approaching one another, and on the right we see Harold, mounted on a black horse, receiving a report from one of his own scouts. Harold's scout goes on foot. He had no horsemen to spare.

ISTE NVNTIAT HAROLDVM REGE DEEXERCITV VVILELMI DVCIS

Harold had hurried back from the Humber with his sadly diminished force of house-carles, exhausted by weeks of marching and hard fighting. He had sent messengers through the countryside summoning feudal levies to meet this new emergency. Contingents of these joined him as he pressed south, but there were many parties that failed to arrive in time. Nevertheless he contrived to raise a sizeable army which may have been numerically larger than that of William. But it was an army of peasants, ill-trained, ill-equipped, and poorly disciplined.

HIC WILLELM:DVX ALLOQVITVR:SVIS:MILITIBVS:VT:PREPARA

The Norman cavalry advances into battle.

William with his mace is evidently exhorting his followers to fight bravely. No doubt he will have reminded them that the blessing of the Church was upon their enterprise; but since many of them were adventurers in search of gain, small landowners from the countries adjoining Normandy who hoped to add to their estates, his pointing finger may well have been directed also to the rich and fertile English countryside, where so much wealth and honour was to be won.

...SE VIRILITER ET SAPIENTER: ADPRELIVM:

The battle has been joined. In the centre of the picture, on the ridge of high ground, which was afterwards given the name of Battle, we see Harold's house-carles grouped tightly together in a "shield-wall" to resist the onslaught of the Norman cavalry. This shield-wall was a fighting formation in which the house-carles were specially trained. And in the centre of the group is a single unarmoured bowman, perhaps put in as a reminder that Harold's army contained only a few archers. The bow had not been adopted as a weapon of war in England at that time, and the light arrows used for hunting could have had little effect against armoured knights.

Scenes of battle. The fighting went on throughout the day, and the makers of the Tapestry have here handed down to us a terrible and wonderful picture of the savagery and confusion of war.

The details do not greatly matter. The two armoured figures so dramatically falling in the early part of the picture are Harold's brothers Leofwyn and Gyrth. The English house-carles are shown using the Danish battle-axe, a weapon that had been adopted in England but which was not used by the Normans. We see the slaughter of horses and a stand by a group of English foot soldiers on a hillock. But it is the vigour and movement of this battle sequence that makes it remarkable; and the lower border lays further stress on the designer's intention, which was to depict the horror of war.

HIC CECI—DERVNT LEVVIN ET:GYRD:FRA

The Tapestry does not attempt to give an exact account of the battle, which lasted for eight hours and developed in several stages. Harold, after occupying the ridge, had intended to advance and attack William's army before it was fully deployed; but when he found that William, anticipating this move, had come out sooner than he had expected, he resolved to fight a defensive battle. William at first held back his knights and attacked with his foot soldiers, who were several times repelled with much slaughter. There was a point when the battle hung in the balance. The Norman left wing, consisting mostly of men from Brittany, had crumpled. If the English had stayed where they were and held their ground, they might have gained the day; but a part of Harold's un-disciplined force, armed with axes and bill-hooks and scythes, broke out of the line against his orders and pursued the fleeing Normans. They were cut off and destroyed.

S:HAROL DI REGIS: HIC CECI DERVNT SIMVL:ANGLI

ET FRANCI:INPRELIO:· HIC·ODO·EP

At one moment a rumour swept through the Norman army that William had been wounded.
We see him amid the cluster of horsemen on the left of the picture,
raising his helmet to show his face and prove that he is unharmed.
Immediately in front of him rides a knight carrying the Papal Banner.

The figure with the mace on the left of the picture is Bishop Odo rallying the younger horsemen, not all of whom were fully-fledged knights. Since the Tapestry was being made at Odo's instructions, it was no doubt considered polite to mention him whenever possible.

The death of Harold. We see him in the lower picture being struck by a rider with a sword; and since the Latin inscription immediately above him says, "Harold the king is killed," there can be no doubt as to who the falling figure is meant to be. Here there is a great question mark. Many history books say that Harold was killed not by a blow with a sword but by an arrow that pierced his eye. This story, whether it is true or not, is among the most widely believed in all the history of the English people.

Yet there are good grounds for supposing that the story is not true and was in fact based at a later date on a misreading of the Tapestry. Not until the twelfth century, long after the event, do we hear any mention of the arrow. There are two Englishmen depicted in the group, one at either end of the horse. The one on the left is plucking an arrow from his eye, while the one on the right is falling beneath the sword. It must be said that the left-hand figure looks by far the nobler of the two. It seems to have been assumed (and we would like to think it so) that *both* figures represent Harold, who after plucking out the arrow continued his heroic but unavailing struggle until he was eventually struck down. But there is no other case in the Tapestry in which two figures representing the same person are included in one small group, nor would this have conformed to the general custom. It seems likely that if this is what the designer intended, he would have found some way of making his intention clear. We do not know. All this was nine centuries ago, and the truth of the matter is lost in time.

RVNT : QVI ERANT : CVM hAROLDO :: hIC

hARO L D : REX : INTERFEC TVS EST

We see the last stages of the battle: the Normans riding on in triumph; and beyond the tree the English, those that were left, scattering over the countryside to return to their cottages and fields. The Latin inscription following the death of Harold simply says, "... and the English turned and fled." There is no more to say. The Norman invasion had succeeded, and Duke William was master of the English realm.

There is reason to suppose that the original Tapestry did not end quite so abruptly, and that its concluding scenes may have been lost. It seems likely, indeed, that it would have been concluded in a more solemn and splendid manner, perhaps with the crowning of William at Westminster. And perhaps also something would have been done to point the moral of the story as the Normans tell it: the tragic doom that befell a great and gallant warrior who broke his sacred oath.

Another thing that may strike us, surveying the story as a whole, is the part that chance played in the business— above all the chance of weather. If the wind had favoured William as soon as his force was assembled, he would undoubtedly have taken advantage of it to set sail perhaps

six weeks earlier than he did. In that event, he would have encountered Harold's full force both by sea and by land and would in all likelihood have been defeated. There would have been no Norman conquest of England, and the history of the English people would have been profoundly changed: whether for better or for worse no man can say.

# Acknowledgements

The authors wish to make warm acknowledgement to the editor and compilers of the splendid comprehensive Survey of the Bayeux Tapestry (Phaidon Press, 1957), which so meticulously and authoritatively covers the whole subject; and also to Miss Hope Muntz, whose novel *The Golden Warrior* brilliantly evokes the feeling of the period. Other works consulted include: F. R. Fowke, *The Bayeux Tapestry* (London, 1898); Hilaire Belloc, *The Book of the Bayeux Tapestry* (London, 1914); *The Anglo-Saxon Chronicle* ('D' version, ed. E. Classen and Florence E. Harmer, Manchester, 1926); the Cambridge Medieval History.

THE LIBRARY
COLLEGE OF FURTHER EDUCATION
NORTHAMPTON

ENGLAND

MONT ST MICHEL

DINAN

BRITTANY

RIVER
COUESNON

RENNES